This book is about *my mother* and her
great-granddaughter. It was written
to capture the eternal love that exists
between a grandparent and grandchild.

Gini and I would like to dedicate this book
to our beloved Mothers and Grandmothers.

Other Bestmann/Bunnell books:
"Where Does God Sleep, Momma?"
"Plant Your Dreams, My Child"

Printed and Bound in Mexico

College Press Publishing Company
Joplin, Missouri
International Standard Book Number: 0-89900-816-X

Nana, Will You Write Me From Heaven?

written by
Nancy Bestmann

illustrated by
Gini Bunnell

Katilin dearest Katilin,
I'm glad you came today.
You bring the sunshine to my heart,
you chase the clouds away.

I feel just like a child
again when you are
by my side.
The world is so much
nicer when I see it
through your eyes.

But we must talk,
 dear Katie, for Grandma's
 getting old.
And one day I will not be
 here; to heaven
 I will go.

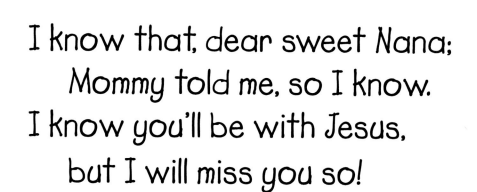

I know that, dear sweet Nana;
Mommy told me, so I know.
I know you'll be with Jesus,
but I will miss you so!

Of course I'll write
you, Katie, I'll write
you
every day.

I'll let you know
that I am fine
but in a special
way.

When you hear bluebirds
singing, high up in
the trees...

they'll be telling
you that I am fine
and happy
as can be.

At night when stars are twinkling
and dancing in the sky,
I'll be dancing with the angels
in heaven oh so high.

And when I have a
message that's filled
with all *my* love,
you'll feel a warm glow
deep inside as I
send it from
above.